Sewing Clothes for Barbie

Making Clothing for Your Child's Barbies Can Be Fun and Easy

DEDICATION

Contents

Barbie Cap Sleeve Shirt

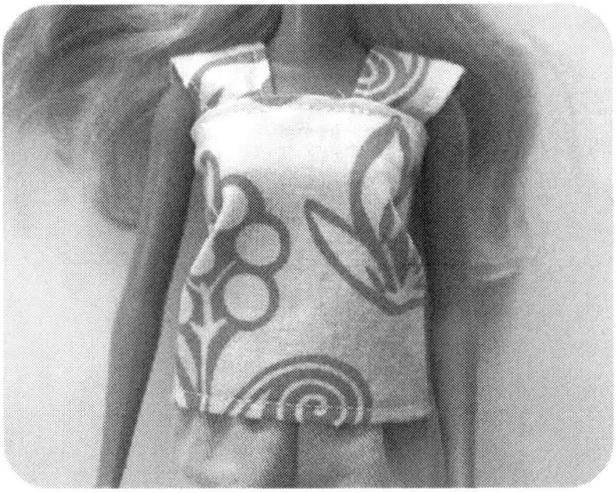

YOU'LL NEED:

one 6 1/2" x 3" piece of fabric

two pieces of fabric 3"x1 1/2", one side cut on a slight curve

sew on velcro, sewing stuff

INSTRUCTIONS:

1. First, serge or zig zag stitch around all edges.

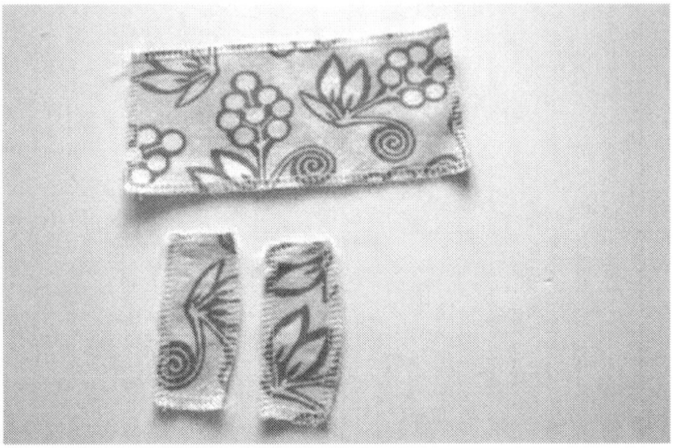

2. Then With Your Iron, Press All Edges In 1/4 Inch. On The Sleeve Pieces, Only the long sides need to be pressed in.

3. Sew around the large piece with about 1/8" seam.
4. (Are You Still singing that song from Mulan in your head? I am.)

5. Also Sew Along the long sides of the sleeve pieces.

6. Hey doll! How's it goin'. Now here's where you can make the top more fitted, or leave it loose-your preference!

7. Wrap the large piece, inside out around her torso, and pin the back together so it's snug. Then, form little darts and pin them like so.

8. Back stitching at start and finish, sew along the pins.

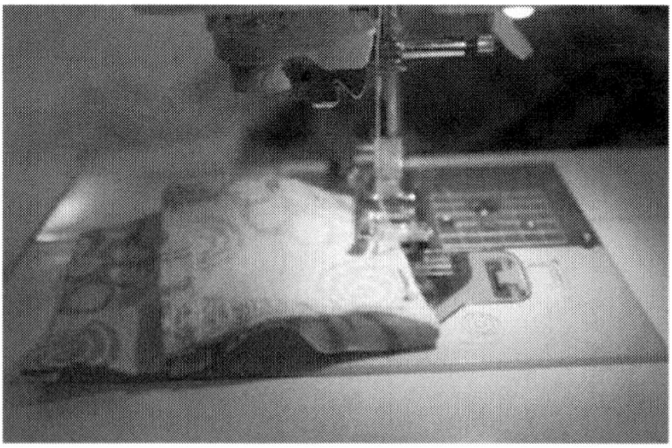

9. Make Sure it fits…..this isn't the best dart job. sorry.

10. Take your sleeves and pin them into place on the front and back.

11. Sew Them on, using your stitching as a guide, back stitch at start and finish.

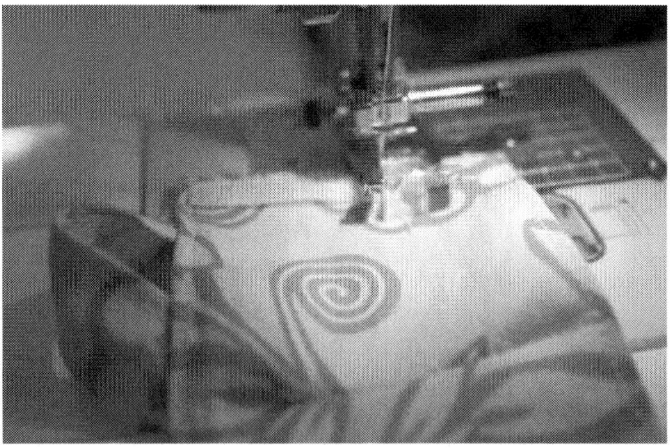

12. Cut A piece of sew on velcro to fit, and sew it on!

Basic Easy Dress

YOU'LL NEED:

fabric: 1 piece 6 " by 2.5" for the bodice, and 1 piece 5" by 12" for the skirt

ribbon: 2 pieces-2.5" long for straps if you want them

sew-on velcro: 4 inches long, and a little over 1/4" wide (i cut 3/4 inch velcro in half)

sewing stuff: thread, iron, scissors, sewing machine….yada yada

INSTRUCTIONS:

1. First, serge or zig zag all edges of your fabric… and with your iron press the two short sides, and one long side of each fabric piece in 1/4 inch.

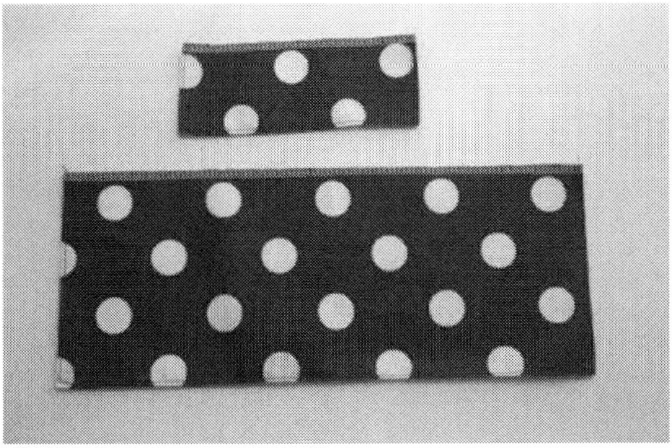

2. Sew about 1/8 inch seam around those three sides.

3. Take your bodice piece, and wrap it around your Barbie® (thanks for modeling for us, Cinderella!)
4. Pin the back together so it's snug, and then pin the front like so for the darts.

5. Sew along the pins for the darts…back stitch a few stitches start and finish so they don't come out! (make sure to use matching thread!)

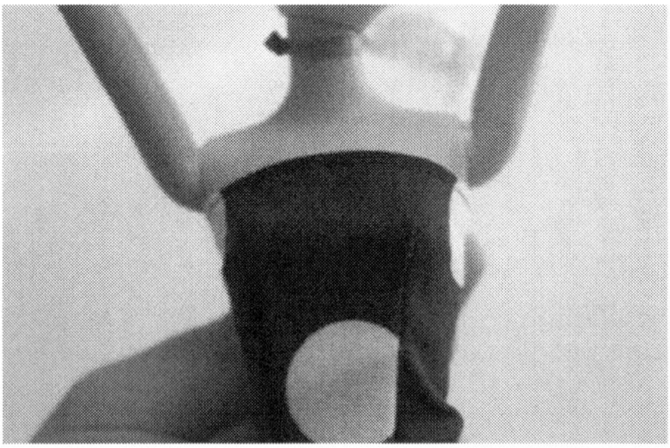

6. Try it on and make sure the darts fit!

7. Sew a basting stitch (longest straight stitch on your machine) along the top of your skirt piece, and pull the top thread to gather.

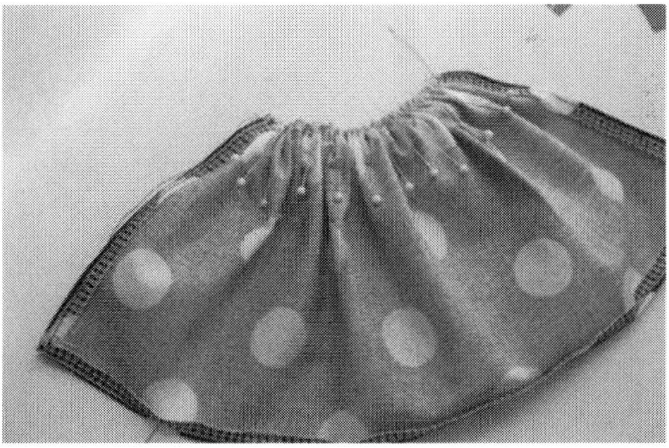

8. Fit it to your bodice piece and pin the heck out of it.

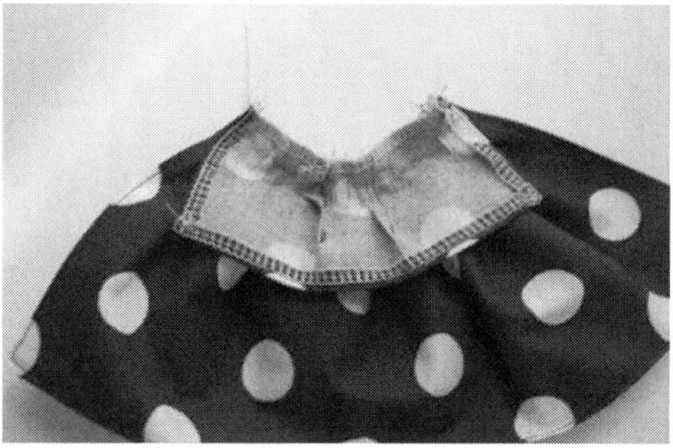

9. (The other side) Now sew those pieces together with about 1/2 inch seam. finish that seam-serge or zig zag stitch.

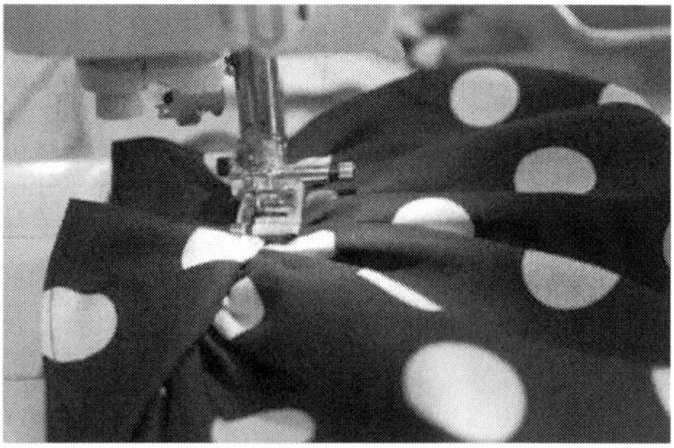

10. Turn over to the right side, press with your iron, and then sew a top stitch (1/8" from the edge) right along your seam.

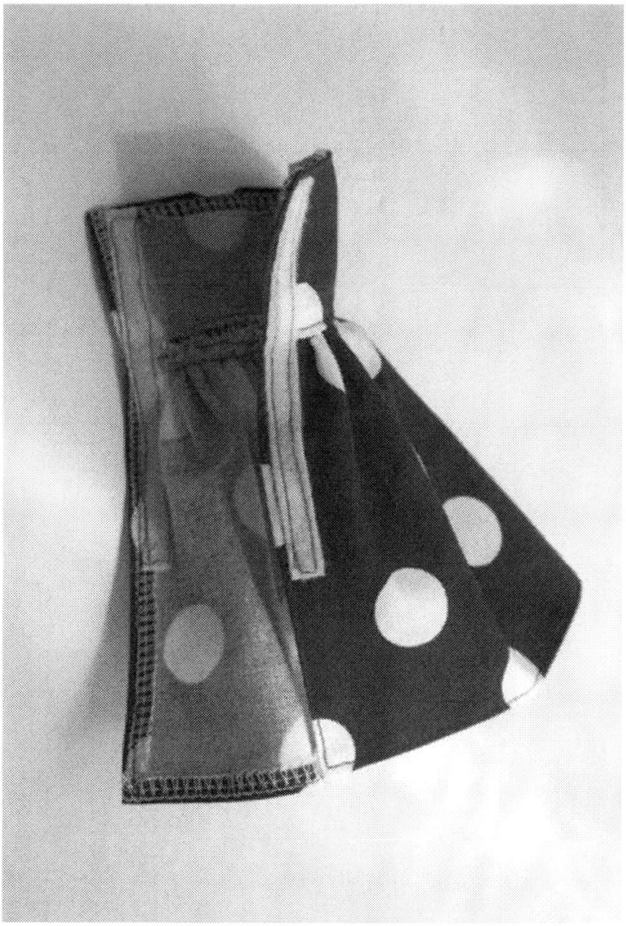

11. Then sew on your velcro pieces!

12. Tada! Doesn't cinderella look so fashionably retro?

13. Love it.

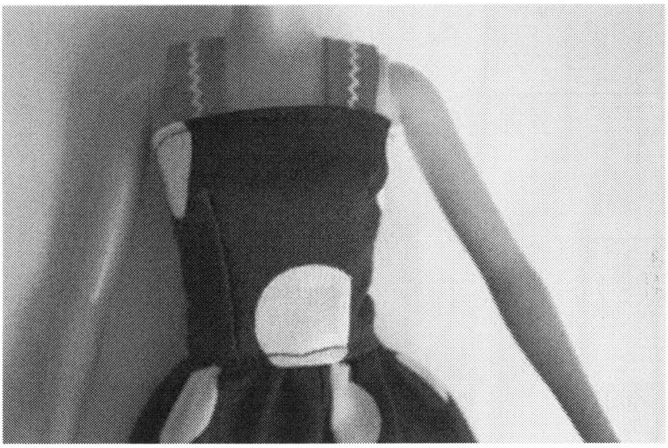

If you'd like straps…sew on your ribbon straps like so…I just placed mine for the picture, I ended up liking the strapless, even though it's a bit scandalous! I will probably sew on some cap sleeves so she can be modest..(tutorial for that tomorrow)..that's the great thing about this-it's so easily customizable!

Here's a version with a ribbon belt and matching straps. ca-ute!

Froufy Barbie Skirt

YOU'LL NEED:

1 piece of fabric 12"x3.5" (for the length shown here)

1 piece of fabric 1.25"x5" for the waistband

sew on velcro

sewing stuff

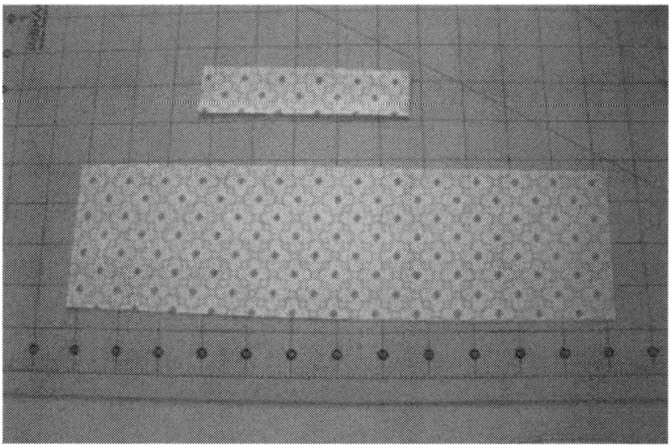

INSTRUCTIONS:

1. Cut your pieces out-I'm not sure how my skirt piece ended up crooked-whatevs!

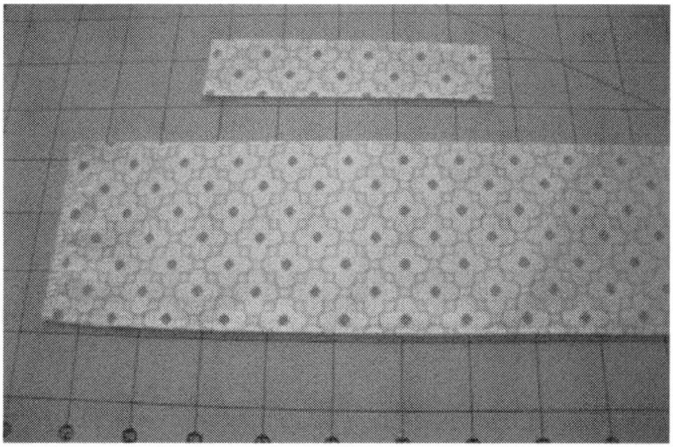

2. Serge or zig zag stitch two short sides, and one long side of your skirt piece. Hem the bottom by folding up 1/4" and

sewing down.

3. On the other side of your skirt piece, sew a basting stitch down the edge, and gather to fit the waistband.

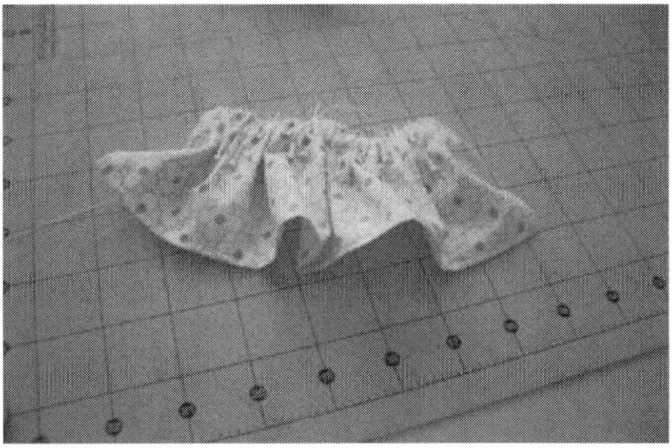

4. Important! Pin your waistband right side to the wrong side of the skirt, matching up the edges.

5. Andd…sew together! with about an 1/2 inch seam.

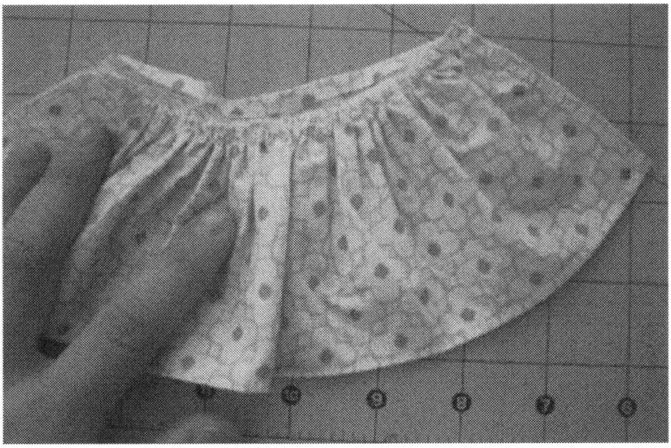

6. Press the waistband, folding a little bit over like so.

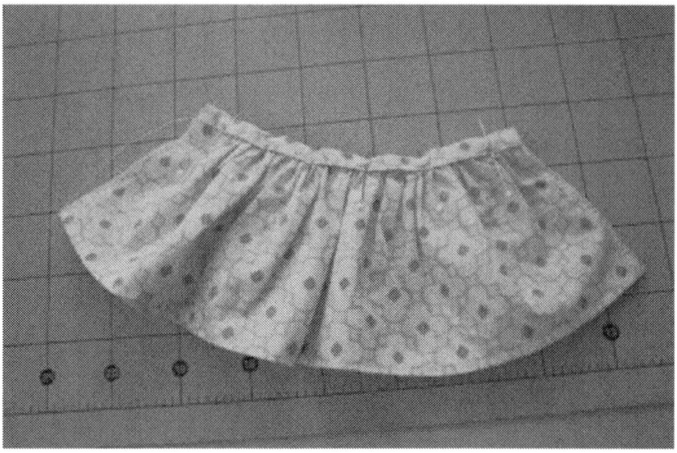

7. Fold that down over the front of your skirt-and pin.

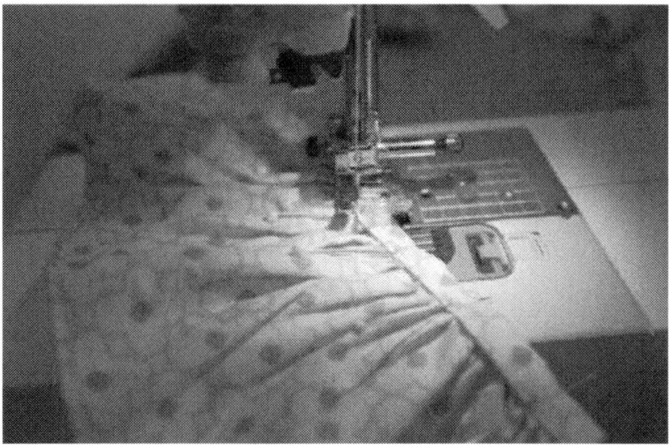

8. Topstitch slowly along the bottom of the waistband. Zig zag stitch or serge the edges again where your waistband is to minimize fraying.

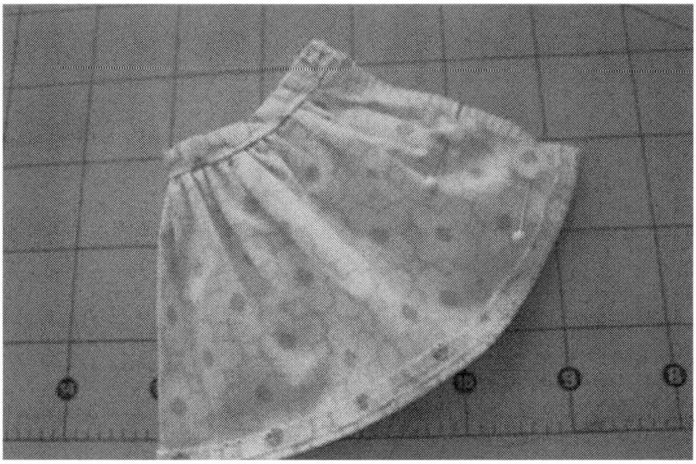

9. Pin right sides together, and sew a seam about an inch from the bottom down…

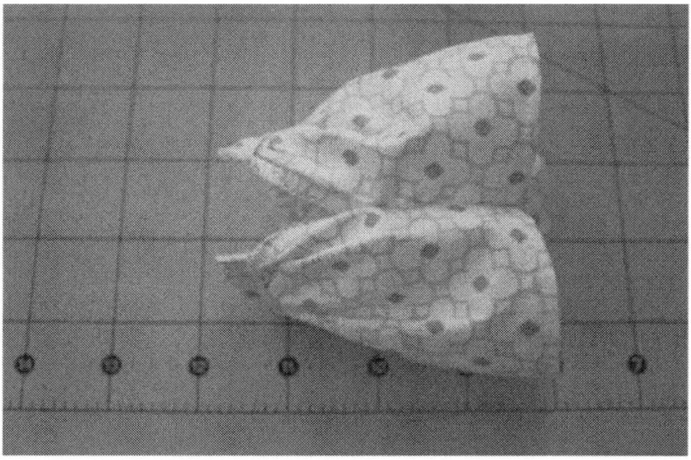

10. This is what it should look like.

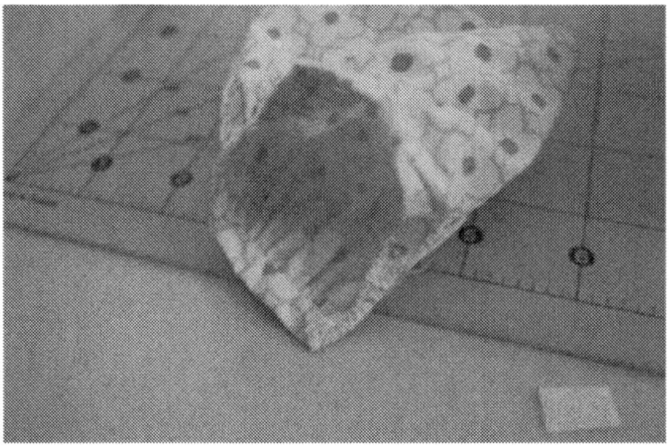

11. fold over one of the edges slightly, sew down, and then sew on your velcro pieces.
12. And tada! Barbie® has a new fun skirt!

Easy Barbie Skirt

YOU'LL NEED:

one piece of fabric 7 1/2" x 4 1/2", or two pieces equaling that, if you want the pieced look. (of course you can go longer or shorter)

a piece of 1/4 inch elastic 4 inches long

INSTRUCTIONS:

1. Sewing stuff-matching thread

2. Sew or serge your two pieces right sides together like so…
3. Serge or zig zag stitch the other two long edges, and hem your bottom piece.

4. **Use your matching thread for this step-or as close of a match as you can get**
5. Then on the other edge, lay your elastic down about 1/2 inch

from the edge, stitch and back stitch a few times.

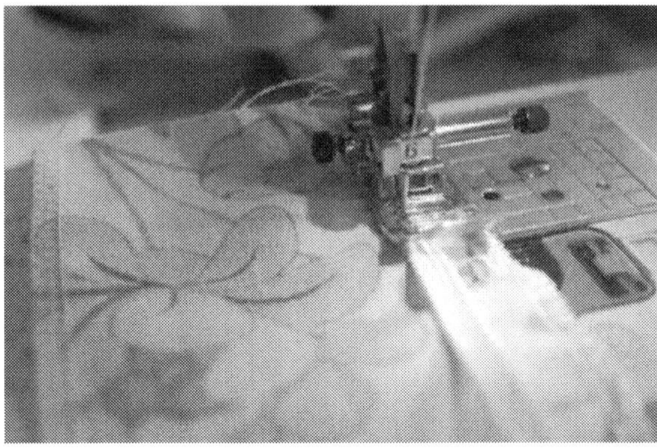

6. Then start stitching along your elastic, stretching it towards you as you go. It gets easier once you can help it through the other way. Just don't tug backwards too hard, be gentle on your machine!

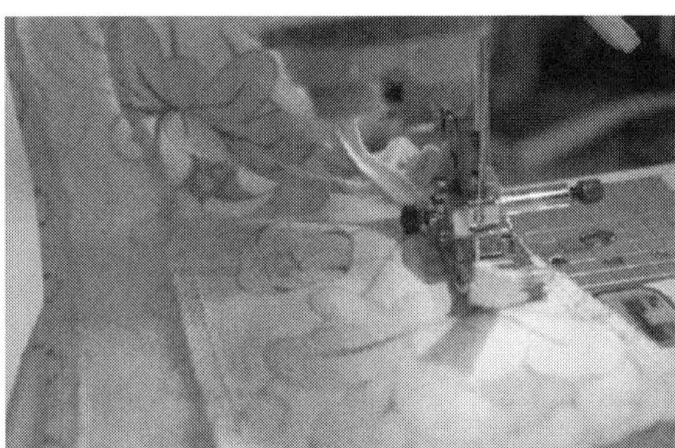

7. Keep going until you reach the end…it should just about fit, if not, snip off the extra fabric. Back stitch a few times as well.

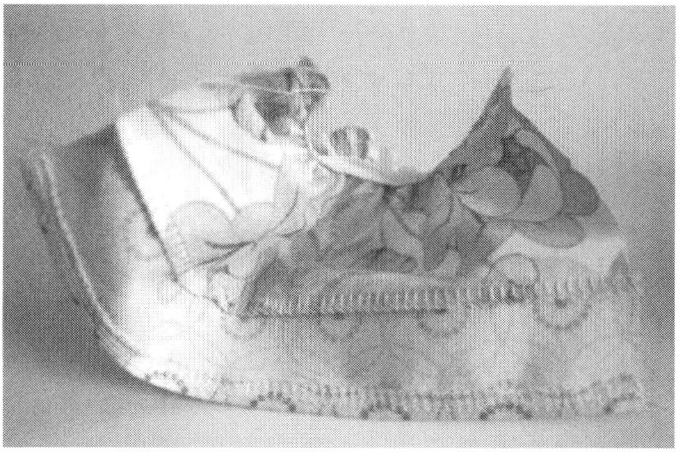

8. This is what you should have. cute, huh?

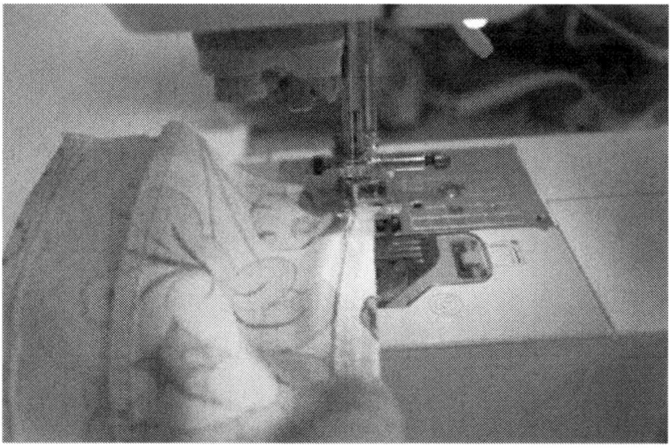

9. Next, fold the top over the elastic, and sew along the edge, forming your waistband.

10. Tada!

11. Then, match up your seams right sides together, pin together…

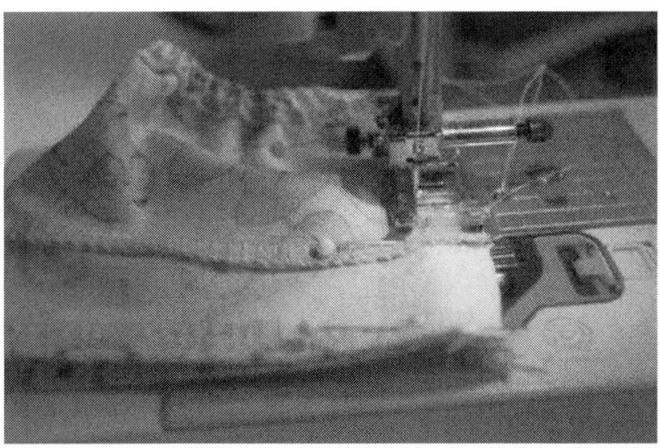

12. And sew with about 1/2" seam

13. Serge or zig zag the seam. Press with your iron.

14. You're done!

Barbie Apron

INSTRUCTIONS:

1. Cut one apron body and one rectangle 20" x 1-1/2" for the waistband/ties.

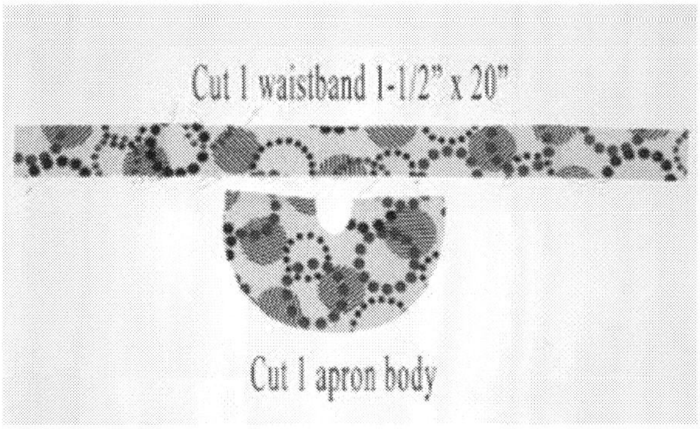

2. Pin the lace trim on the right side of the apron matching the bottom edge. Stitch using a 1/4" seam allowance.

3. The lace trim after it's stitched to the apron.
4. Turn the bottom edge towards the wrong side of the apron. Lightly press.

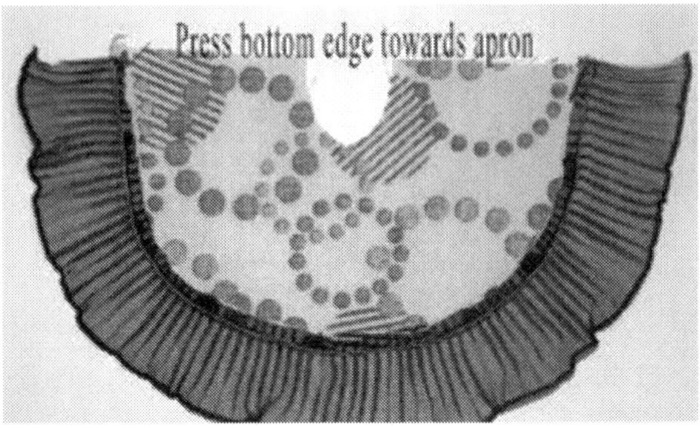

5. On the right side stitch close to the edge which will hold the hem in place.

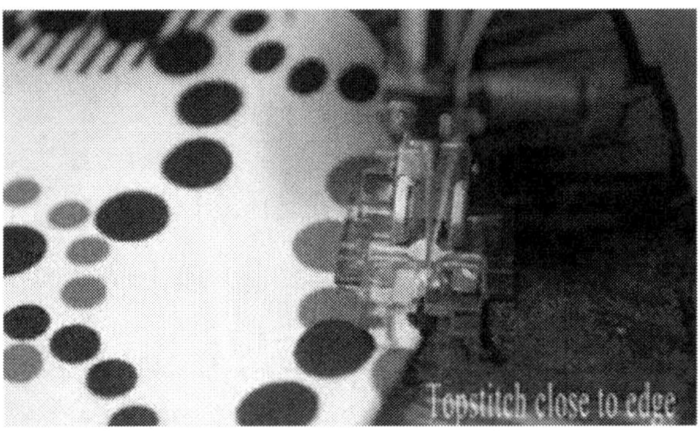

6. Fold the back edge toward the wrong side by 1/4". Finger press. Fold another 1/4" toward the wrong side. Press.

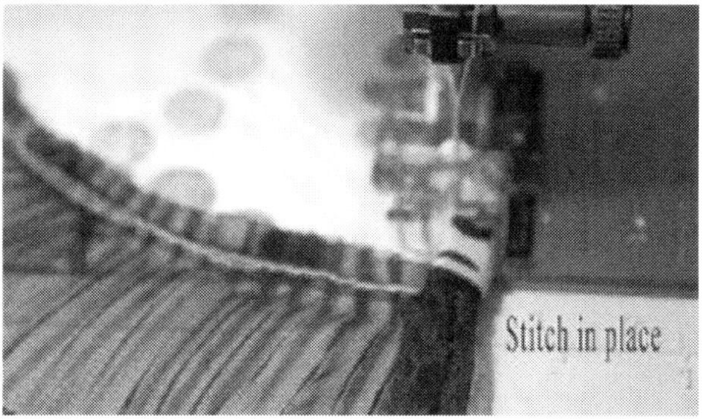

7. Stitch side hem in place.

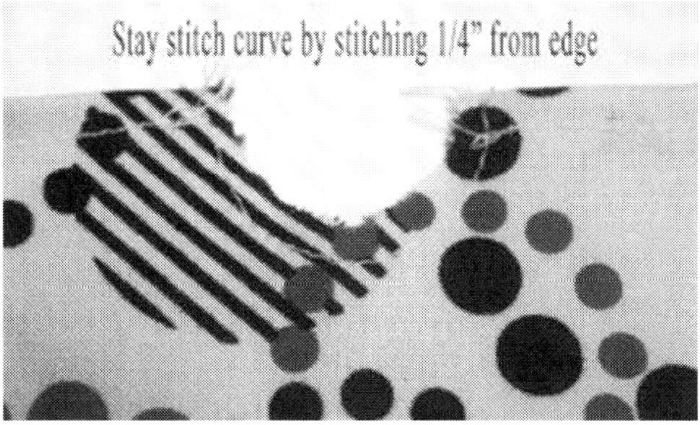

8. Staystitch the waist curve by stitching 1/4" from the edge.

Carefully clip curves to stitches

9. Carefully clip to the stitching. Don't worry if you accidentally clip through the stitches , just restitch.
10. Mark the center of the waistband using a removable fabric marker or chalk.

11. Pin the wrong side of the apron to the right side of the waistband matching center.

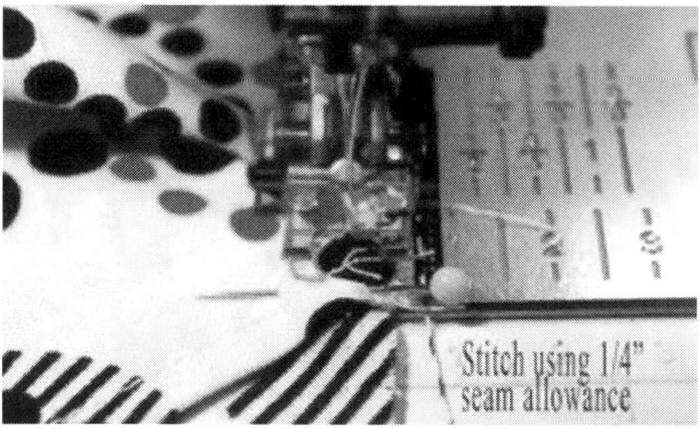

12. Stitch the apron to the waistband using a 1/4" seam allowance.

13. Press the seam toward the waistband.

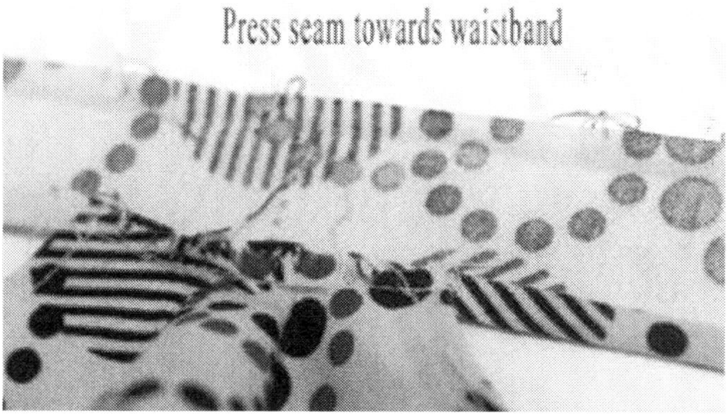

14. Continue pressing the long edge of the waistband 1/4" toward the wrong side of the waistband.

15. Press the other long edge and both short ends of the waistband 1/4" toward the wrong side of the waistband.

16. Fold the waistband in half wrong sides together. Pin in place over the apron seam.

17. Stitch close to the edges of the waistband being sure to secure the waistband to the apron.

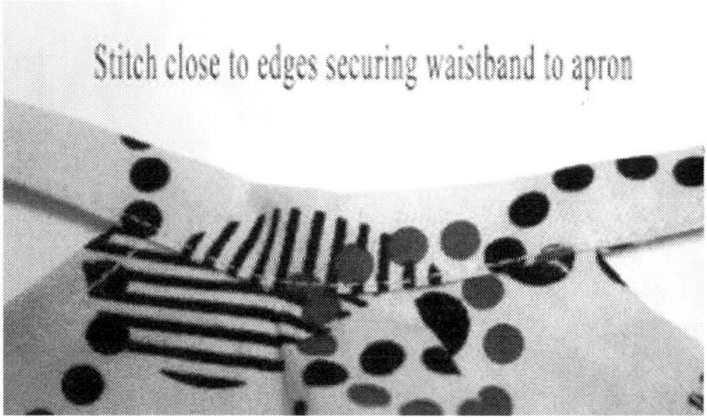

18. Tie apron on your Barbie and admire.

Fashion Doll Trench Coat

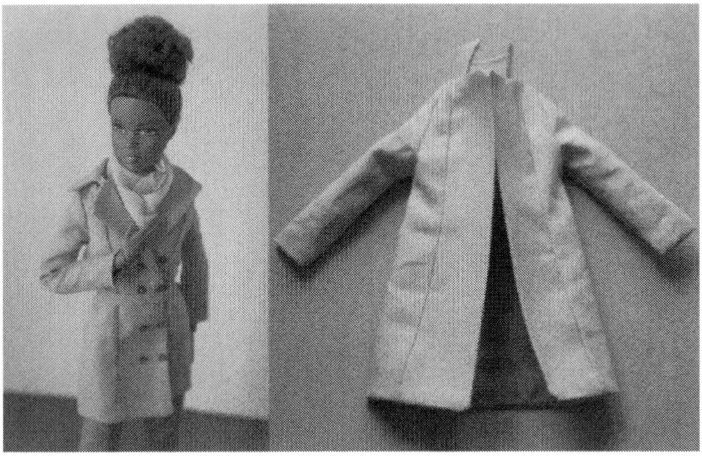

INSTRUCTIONS:

1. Cut pattern pieces from your main fabric: back – 1 piece, side back – 2 pieces, side front – 2 pieces, front – 2 pieces, sleeve – 2 pieces.

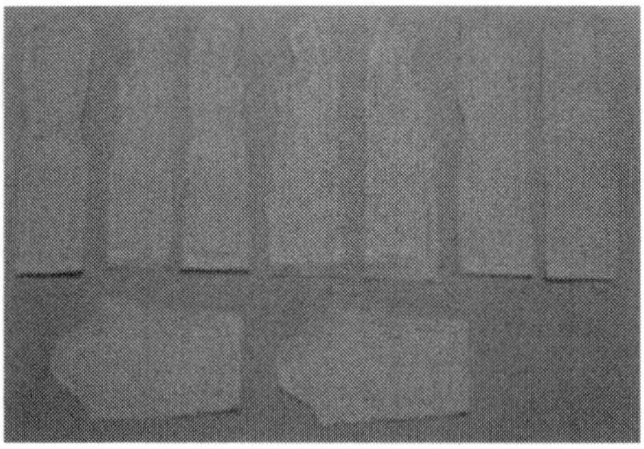

2. Cut 2 front facing pieces from main fabric.

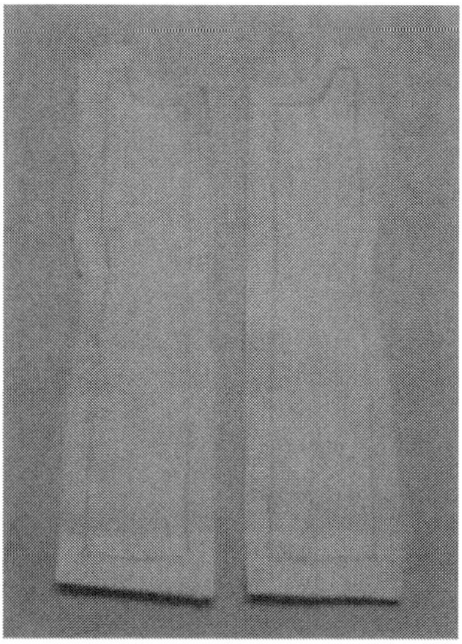

3. Cut pattern pieces from your lining fabric: back – 1 piece, side back – 2 pieces, sleeve – 2 pieces.

4. Sew the main fabric pieces of front and back and iron the seams.

Sew shoulder seams and iron.

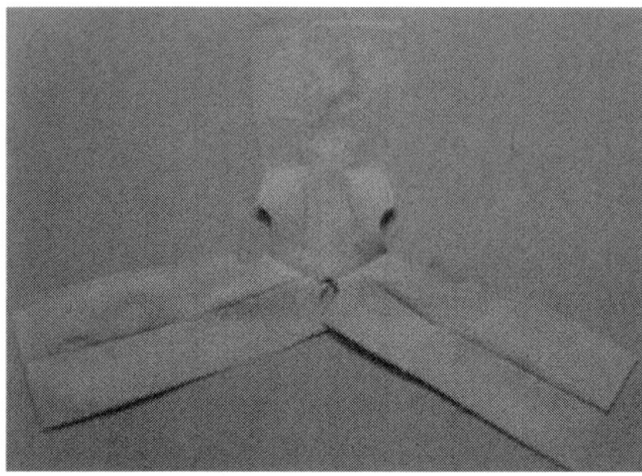

5. Repeat all steps in lining parts.

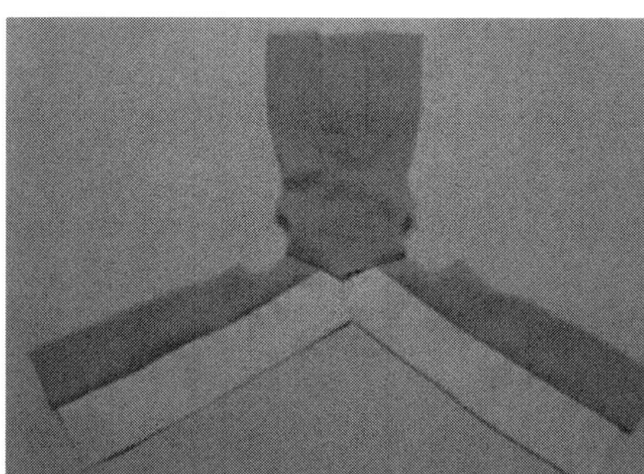

Sew the sleeve cap to the armhole.

6. Cut out the collar. I drew it by sight.

Add a hemming tape.

Turn the collar and press for the parts of the collar to be glued together.

7. Hand-baste the collar and the neckline of the bodice.

8. Sew the garment shell and the lining with right sides together and the collar inside. I start sewing with the neckline to make the thing symmetric.

Trim off the excess.

This is how the collar looks from outside.

8. Stitch the shell sleeve and lining sleeve hem together.

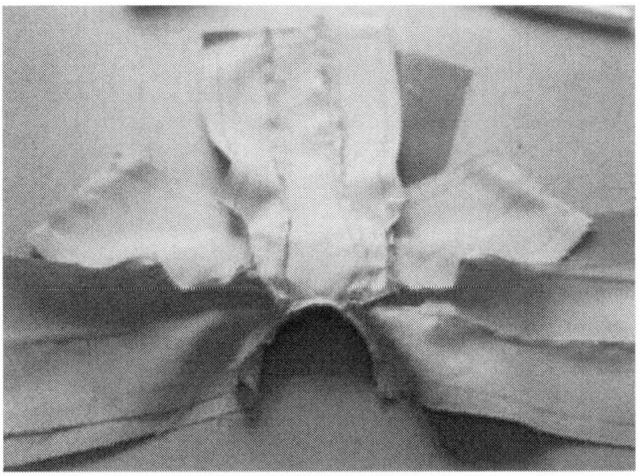

9. Sew the sleeve seams and side seams of the shell. Repeat in lining parts. This is how it should look like:

It seems difficult at first but when you sew the thing for the third time you will understand everything

10. Stitch the front and the facing, then sew the bottom of the coat leaving opening for turning.

11. Glue hemming tape to front facing.

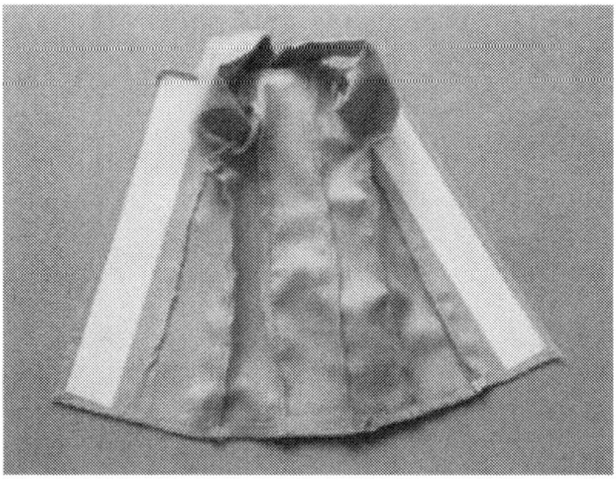

12. Turn the coat.

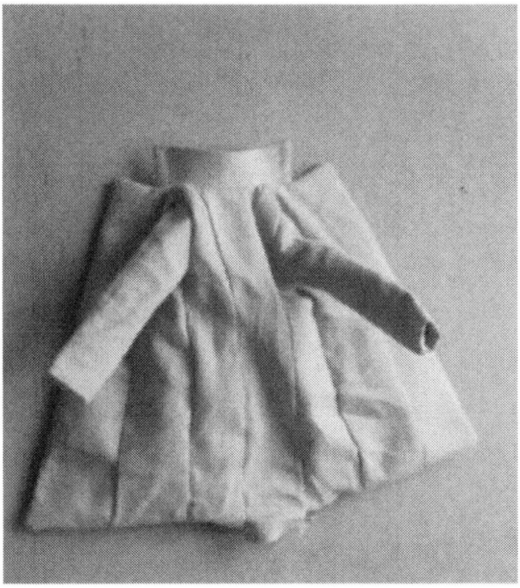

13. Press the coat and sew the bottom edge of the garment.

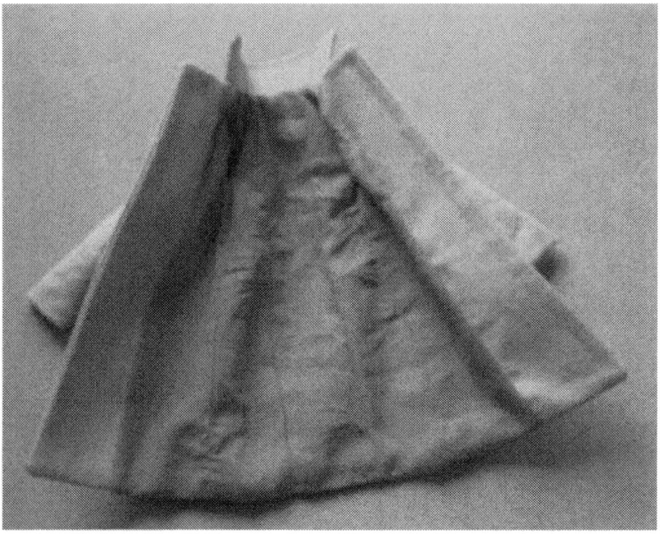

Sew buttons, closure and a belt. Your coat is ready!

Halter Top Dress

INSTRUCTIONS:

1. Fold over sides of both top pieces and topstitch
2. Lay one top piece over the other to the place where the arrow points, pin them together then gather the lower edges of both

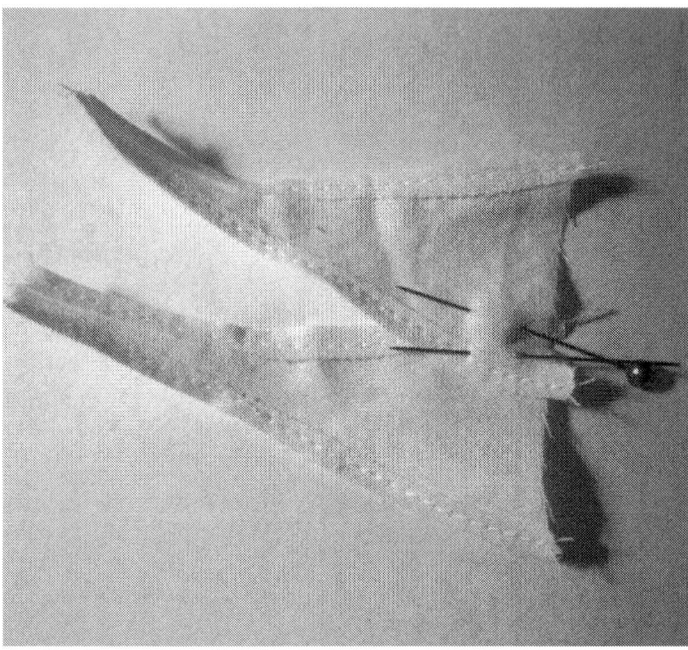

3. Pull gathering threads until the top pieces fit between the two arrows marked on the midriff piece

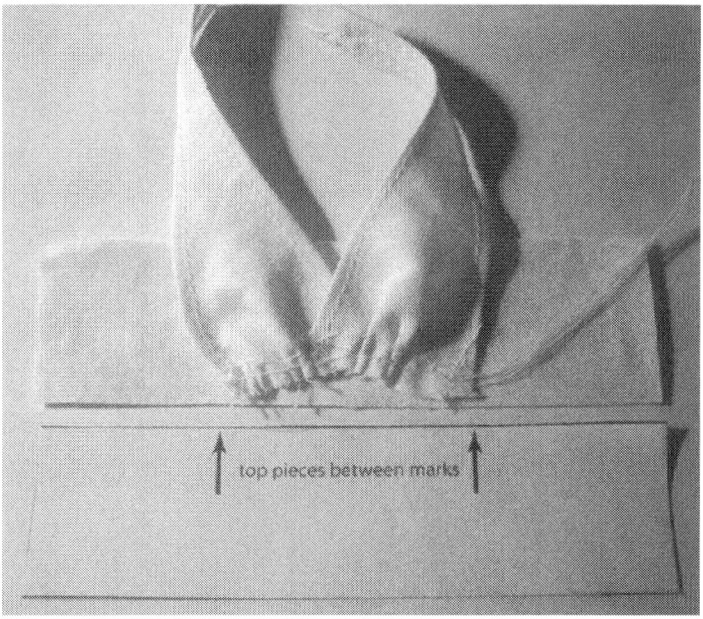

4. Stitch top pieces inside doubled layers of midriff, leaving an opening where the top pieces are, through which you're going to turn the midriff. Clip corners and turn.

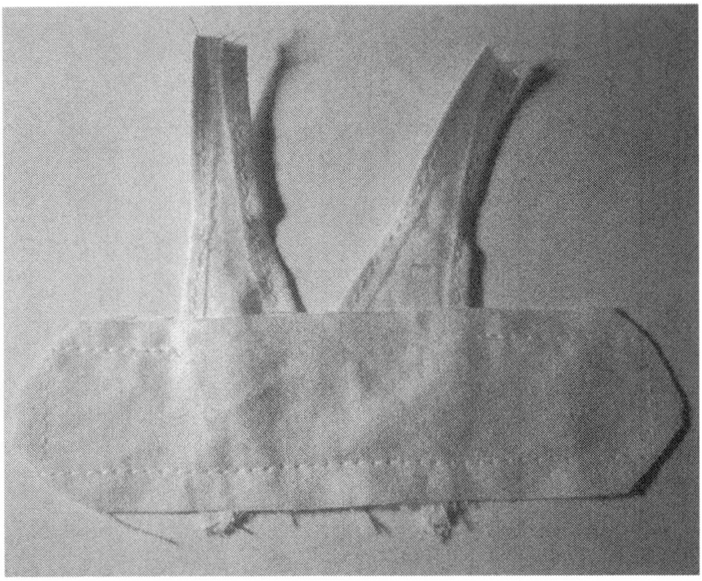

5. Sew skirt side seams, then stitch skirt to midriff, leaving back edges of skirt a little wider than midriff

6. Then fold those over and stitch center backs and hemline

7. Sew on velcro or snaps for closure

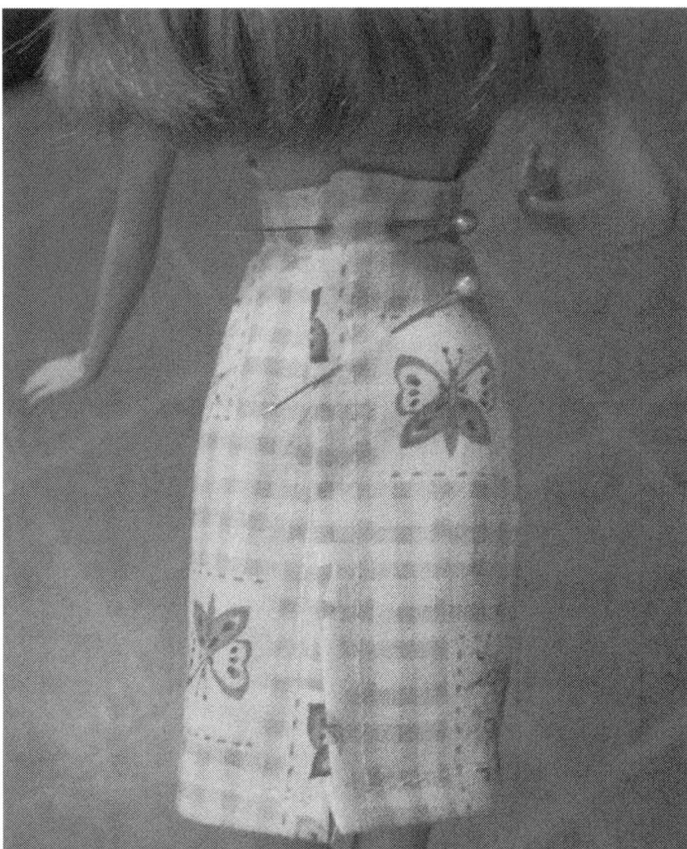

Printed in Great Britain
by Amazon

60265108R00033